Ruby Bridges

by Simone T. Ribke

Content Consultant

Nanci R. Vargus, Ed.D.
Professor Emeritus, University of Indianapolis

Reading Consultant

Jeanne M. Clidas, Ph.D.
Reading Specialist

Children's Press®
An Imprint of Scholastic Inc.
New York Toronto London Auckland Sydney

Library of Congress Cataloging-in-Publication Data
Ribke, Simone T.
  Ruby Bridges/by Simone T. Ribke; poem by Jodie Shepherd.
      pages cm. — (Rookie biographies)
  Includes bibliographical references index.
  Audience: Ages 3-6.
  ISBN 978-0-531-20591-4 (library binding: alk. paper)— ISBN 978-0-531-20993-6
(pbk.: alk. paper)
1. Bridges, Ruby—Juvenile literature. 2. African American children—Louisiana—New
Orleans—Biography—Juvenile literature. 3. African Americans—Louisiana—New
Orleans—Biography—Juvenile literature. 4. New Orleans (La.)—Race relations—
Juvenile literature. 5. School integration—Louisiana—New Orleans—Juvenile
literature. I. Shepherd, Jodie. II. Title.

F379.N59N4447 2015
379.2'63092—dc23 [B]   2014035680

Produced by Spooky Cheetah Press
Poem by Jodie Shepherd
Design by Keith Plechaty

Printed in China 62

SCHOLASTIC, CHILDREN'S PRESS, ROOKIE BIOGRAPHIES®, and associated logos
are trademarks and/or registered trademarks of Scholastic Inc.

7 8 9 10 R 24 23 22 21 20 19 18

Photographs ©: Alamy Images: 27 (Rick Mackler), 28 (SiliconValleyStock); AP
Images: 24 (Steven Senne), 19 (Tim Bath), cover, 15, 16, 31 top, 31 center top; From
the collection of Barbara Henry: 23; Corbis Images/Bettmann: 11, 12, 30 top right, 31
center bottom; Getty Images/Robert W. Kelley: 8, 31 bottom; iStockphoto/fotohorst:
3 bottom; From the collection of Ruby Bridges Hall: 20; The Image Works/Sven
Martson: 4, 30 top left; Thinkstock: 3 top left (Dan Thornberg), 3 top right (Pictac).

Map by XNR Productions, Inc.

Scholastic Inc., 557 Broadway, New York, NY 10012.

Table of Contents

Meet Ruby Bridges

Ruby Bridges became famous when she was only six years old. She was the first African-American student to go to an all-white school in Louisiana.

Ruby was born on September 8, 1954, in Tylertown, Mississippi. She had two younger brothers and a younger sister. Her family moved to New Orleans, Louisiana, when Ruby was four.

MAP KEY

■ Mississippi

● Town where Ruby Bridges was born

Tennessee

Arkansas

Mississippi

AL

Louisiana

Tylertown

New Orleans

Gulf of Mexico

7

At the time, African-American people were treated unfairly in many parts of the country. **Segregation** laws kept black people and white people separate. Things that were meant for black people were not as good as those that white people used. But things were about to change!

This photo shows children in a school for African-American kids.

In 1954, a new law said that schools had to **integrate**. That meant that black children must be allowed to attend white schools. Many white people in the South hated the idea of their children sharing a classroom with black children.

Many white people tried to fight against integration.

A Brave Young Girl

Ruby was chosen to integrate William Franz Elementary School in New Orleans. She would be the only African American in the school. The white parents were very angry. They were ready to do what they could to stop Ruby from coming.

13

Ruby started first grade on November 14, 1960. Angry **protesters** were waiting outside the school when she arrived. Federal marshals had to protect Ruby and her mom as they entered the school.

FAST FACT!

White parents chanted: "Two, four, six, eight, we don't want to integrate!" They threw things at Ruby and her mother.

Once inside the school, Ruby and her mother were taken to the principal's office. They waited there all day. They saw white parents take their children home. The parents chose to keep their kids out of school rather than have them be there with a black child.

On her second day of school, Ruby faced the same screaming parents outside her school. Inside, her new teacher, Barbara Henry, greeted Ruby with a hug. Ruby was Mrs. Henry's only student. There were no other kids in the class.

Mrs. Henry later posed in the classroom she shared with Ruby.

A Hard Year

Ruby was the only student in her class all year. It was not safe for her to eat in the lunchroom or to play outside at recess. Ruby became very lonely. Mrs. Henry ate lunch with her student and tried to make class fun.

The next year, there were more black kids at Ruby's school. The protesters were gone, but so was Mrs. Henry. Ruby always wondered what happened to her teacher.

As time passed, white
children returned to school.

Mrs. Henry

Ruby Grows Up

When she grew up, Ruby married Malcolm Hall and had a family of her own.

In 1995, she reunited with her favorite teacher—Mrs. Henry! They hugged each other like they used to every morning in first grade.

In 1999, Ruby wrote a book about her life called *Through My Eyes*. She also started the Ruby Bridges Foundation. The foundation helps parents and schools work together to end **racism**.

Ruby's book tells about her experience in her own words.

THROUGH
MY EYES

RUBY BR

Timeline of Ruby Bridges's Life

1960
starts first grade

1954
born on September 8

1984
marries Malcolm Hall

Ruby Bridges was a brave little girl who grew into an amazing woman. Her courage helped bring about important changes in the United States. And her story continues to inspire people today.

1995
reunites with Mrs. Henry

1999
starts the Ruby Bridges Foundation

A Poem About Ruby Bridges

Black children in elementary school: zero.

Then six-year-old Ruby became a young hero.

She bravely faced terrible taunting each day,

till little by little, the world turned her way.

You Can Be Courageous

- Do not let the actions or opinions of others affect how you think of yourself.

- If someone is treating you unfairly, speak up.

- Do not give up on something you believe in, even if others try to stop you.

Glossary

integrate (IN-teh-grate): bring two separate things together

protesters (PRO-test-ers): people who show that they disagree with something by marching, carrying signs, or talking about it in public

racism (RAY-sism): hating and treating people unfairly because of their race or religion

segregation (seg-ruh-GAY-shuhn): separating people of different races within a society

Index

Facts for Now

Visit this Scholastic Web site for more information on Ruby Bridges:
www.factsfornow.scholastic.com
Enter the keywords **Ruby Bridges**

About the Author

Simone T. Ribke writes children's books and educational materials. She lives with her family in Maryland.